THE HUMAN BRAIN

BIOLOGY FOR KIDS
Children's Biology Books

BABY PROFESSOR
EDUCATION KIDS

Speedy Publishing LLC
40 E. Main St. #1156
Newark, DE 19711
www.speedypublishing.com

Your brain is the most important organ in your body. It holds your memories and hopes, and evaluates what is going on around you. It is where you decide what you are going to do, and form what you will say. How does your brain do all this? Let's find out!

THE PARTS OF YOUR SMARTS

Medically accurate illustration of the brain.

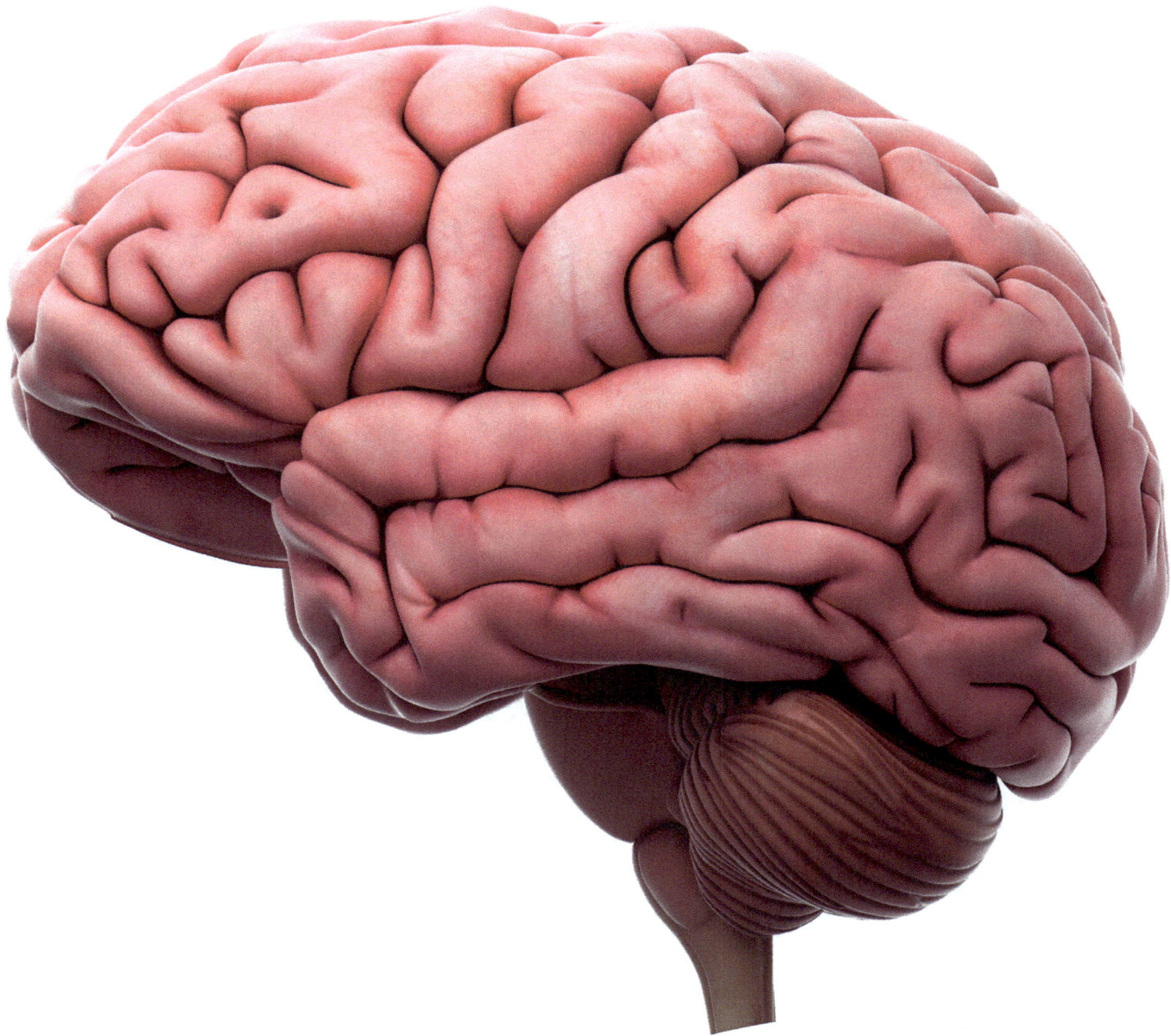

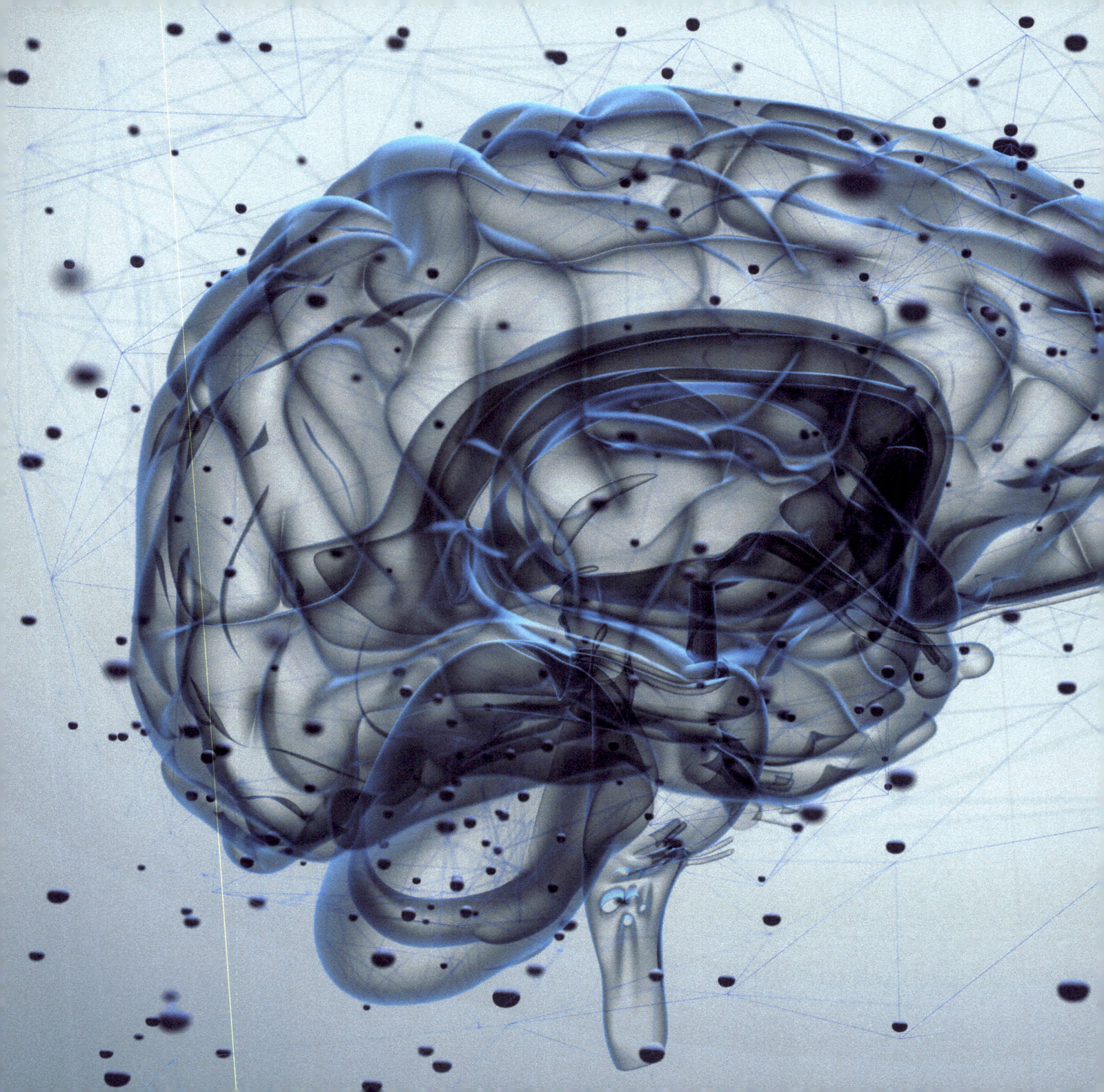

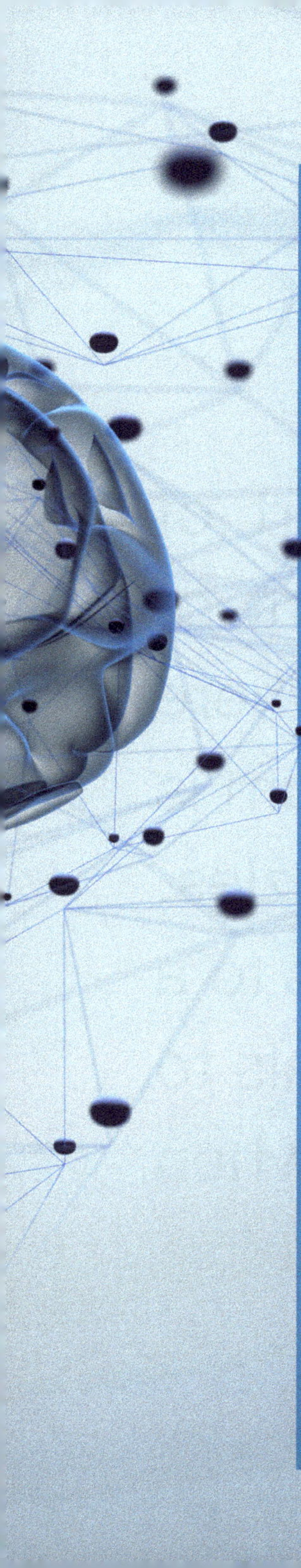

Your brain is one remarkable thinking tool made up of several parts:

- CEREBRUM

- CEREBELLUM

- BRAIN STEM

- HYPOTHALAMUS

- PITUITARY GLAND

- AMYGDALA

Each part has a different job.

Brain activity.

Cerebrum

The cerebrum is the largest part of your brain. It is over 85 percent of the weight of your brain, and it is where your thinking happens. Your cerebrum is where you make plans and solve puzzles, where you try to remember the lyrics to a song, and where you send the signals to tell your hand to pick up your fork when you are eating.

Cerebrum - female brain anatomy lateral view.

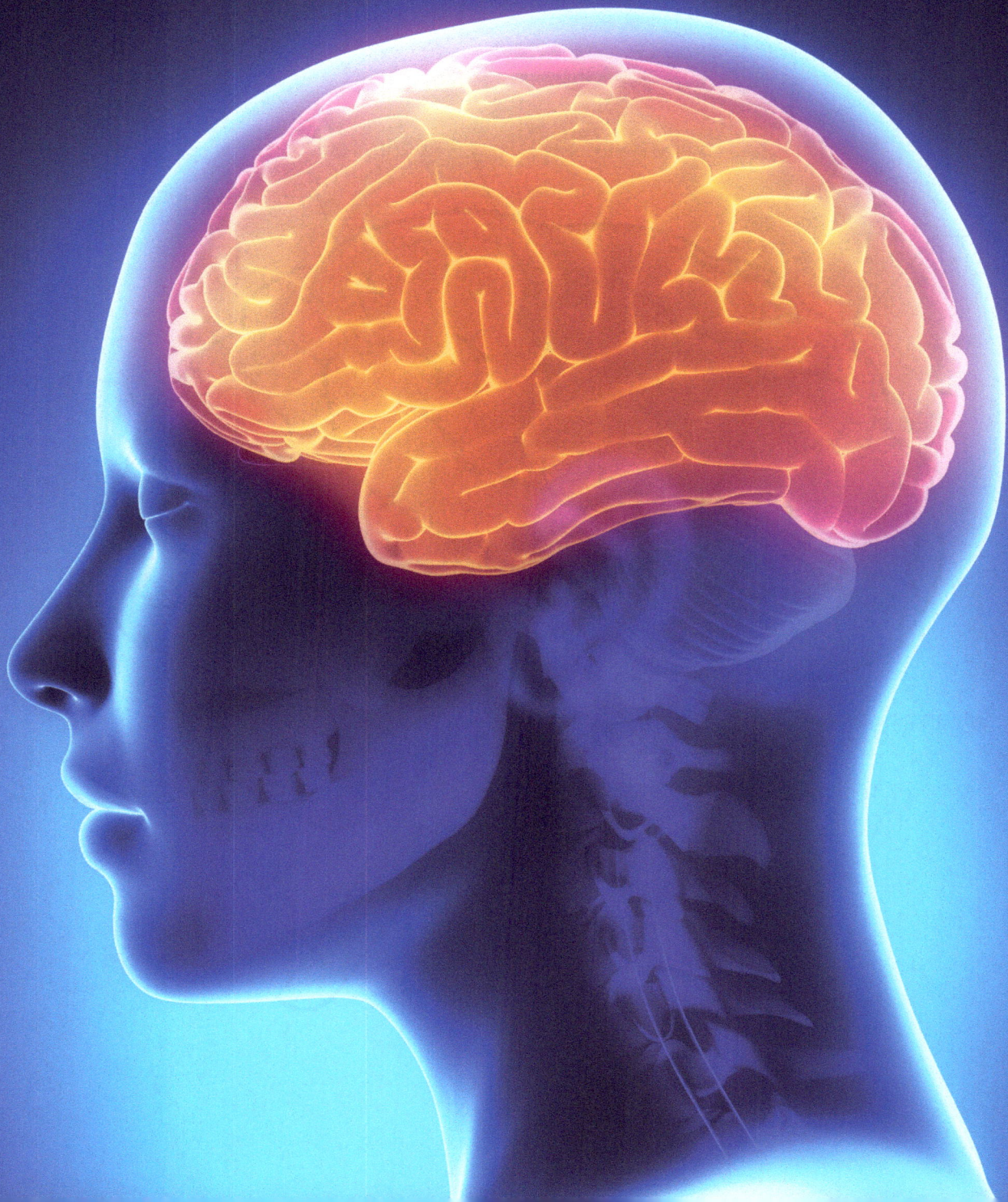

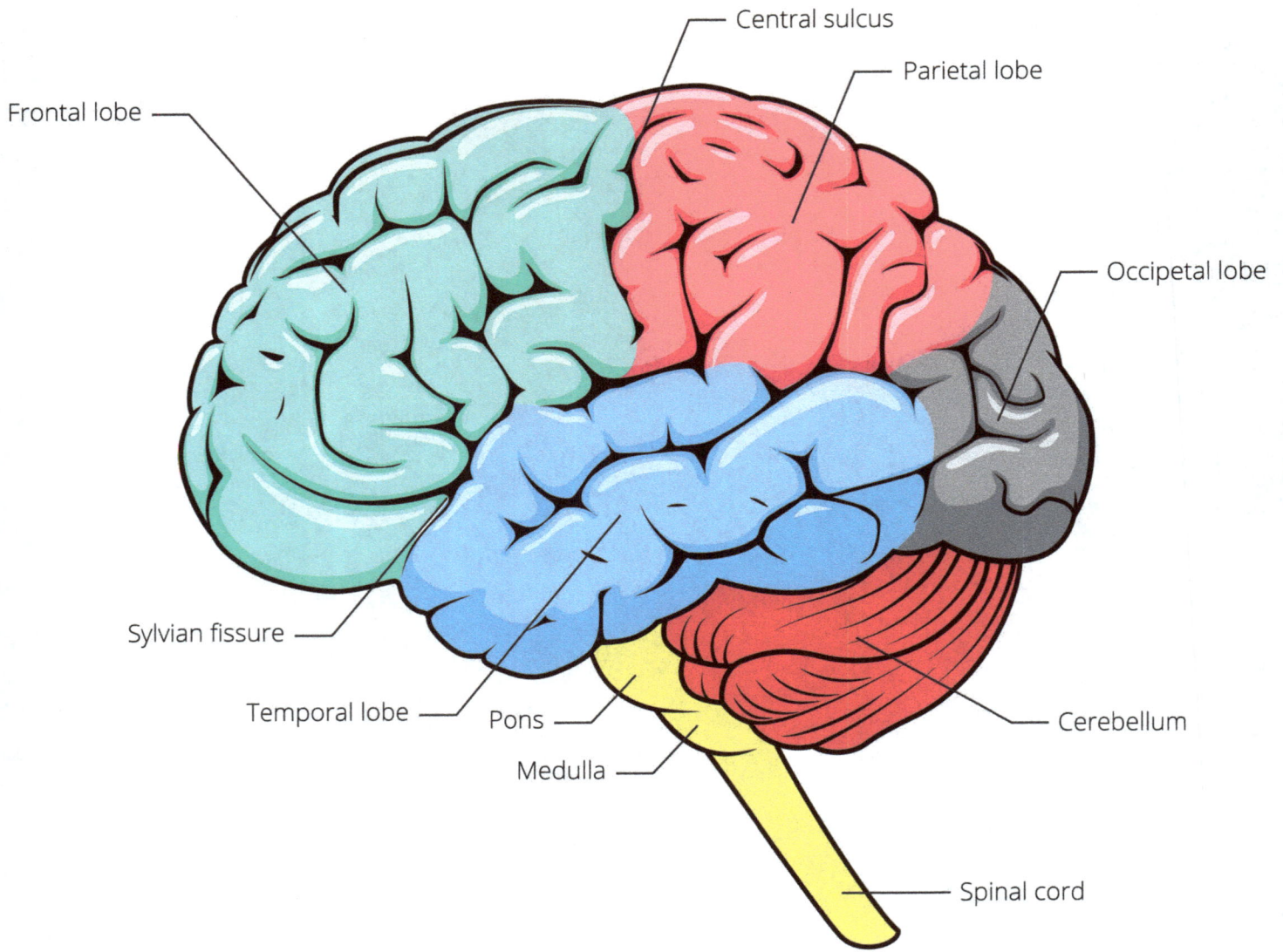

Central sulcus

Parietal lobe

Frontal lobe

Occipetal lobe

Sylvian fissure

Temporal lobe

Pons

Cerebellum

Medulla

Spinal cord

Your cerebrum has a left and right half. Some scientists think the left side of your brain does more with logical things like speech, math, and planning; and that the right side has more to do with things like music, color, and memory. One cool thing is that the right side of your cerebrum controls the voluntary muscles on the left side of your body, and the left side of the cerebrum controls your right side.

Structure of human brain schematic vector illustration.

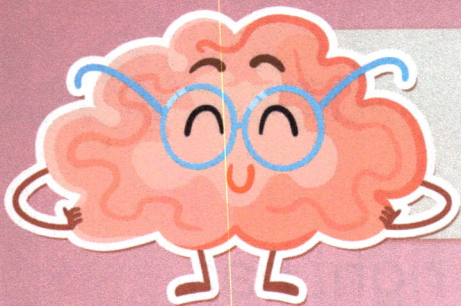

Cerebellum

Your cerebellum is at the back of your head, tucked in under the cerebrum. Here's where your brain takes care of movement, balance, and controlling your muscles so they work together. When you do even simple things like snapping your fingers or tying your shoelaces, your cerebellum is at work, telling each part of your body what to do next. Think of all the work it does when you ride a bike or knit a sweater!

Cerebellum - female brain anatomy lateral view.

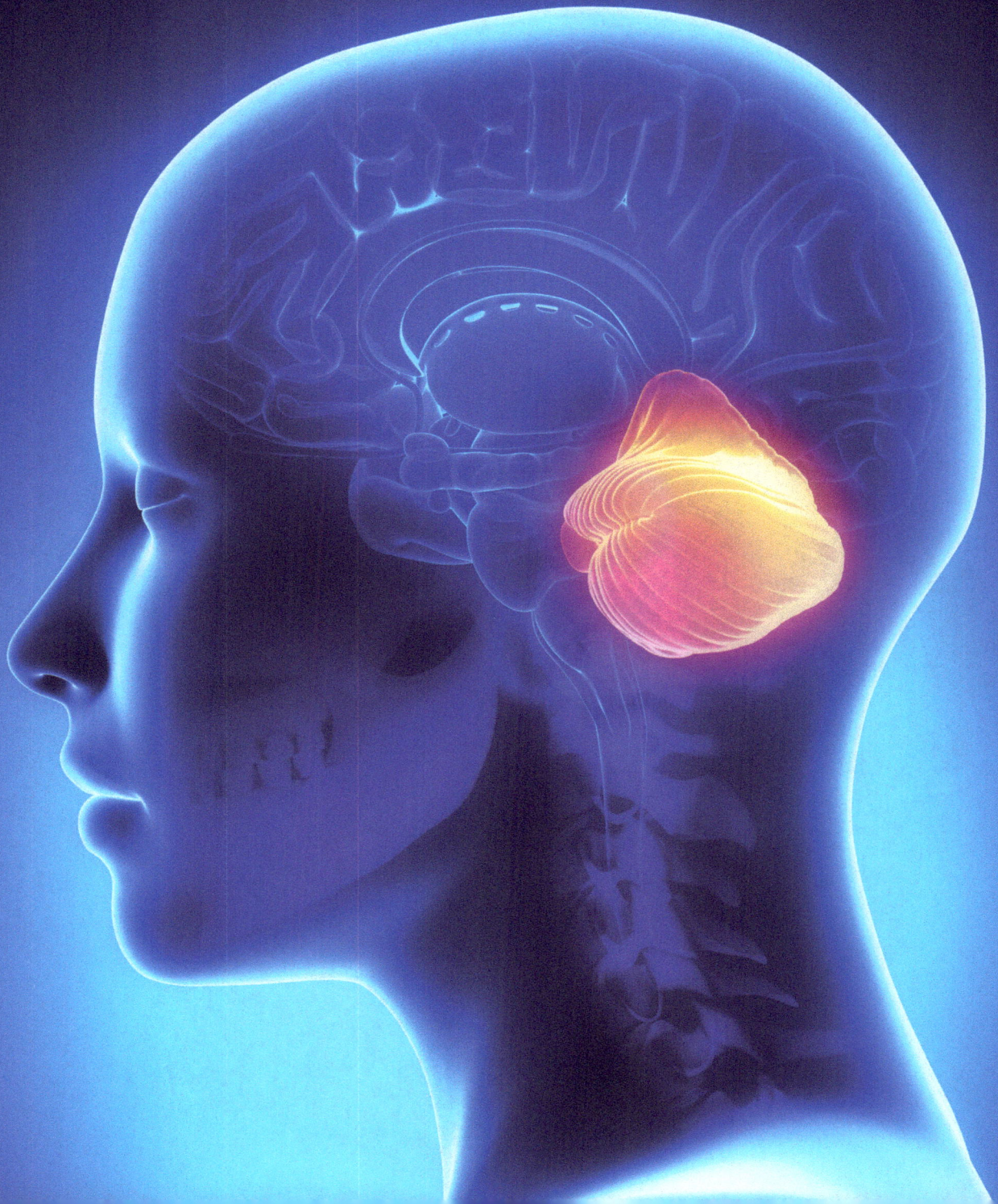

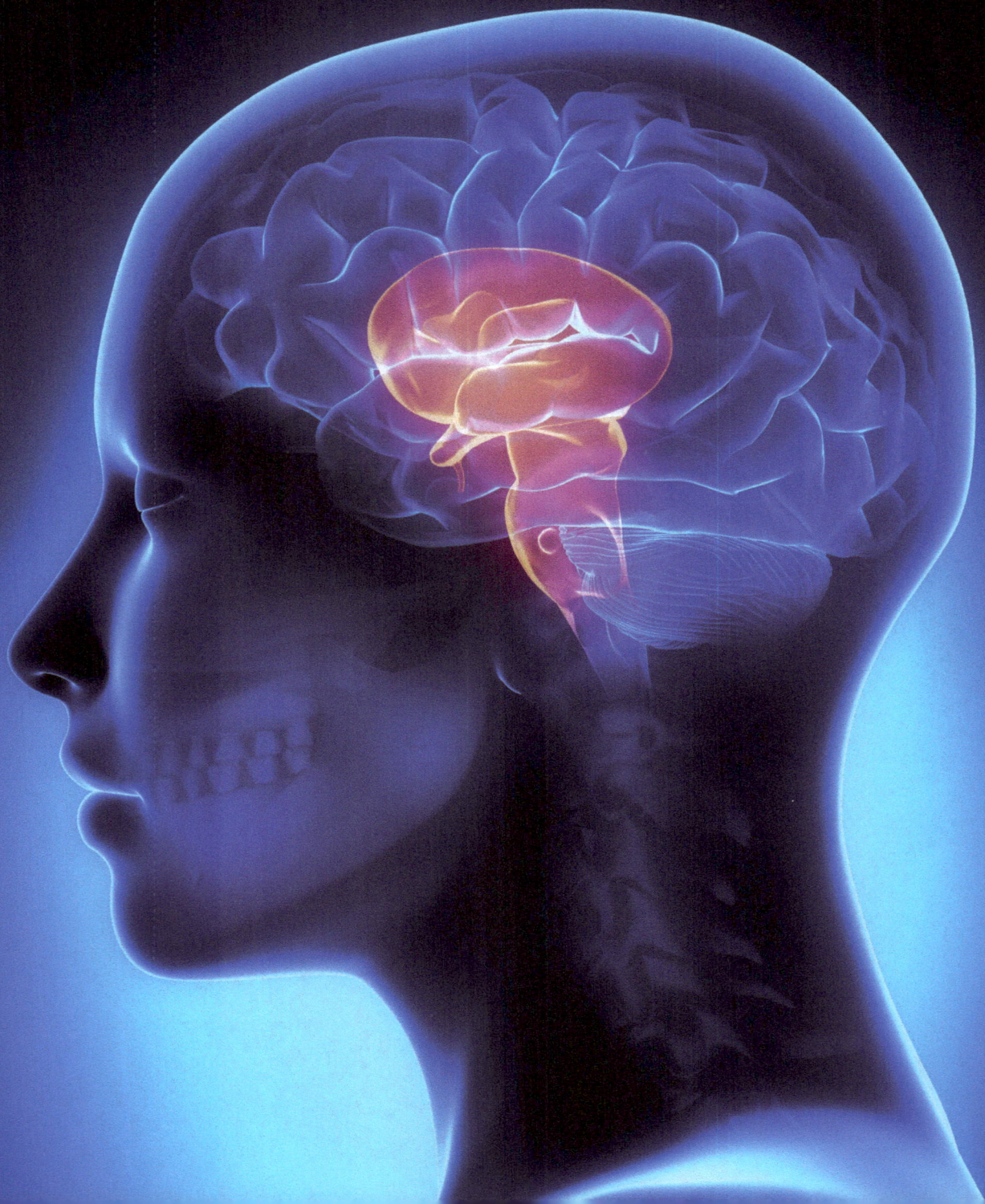

Brain Stem

Your brain stem is in front of the cerebellum, under the cerebrum. This is where your brain connects to your spinal cord. Your spinal cord, protected by your spine, runs from your brain all the way down your back. It connects with the nerves that extend all through your body.

Brain stem - female brain anatomy lateral view.

Most of the messages your brain sends to your body, and the information it gets back, run through the cerebellum and the spinal cord. The exceptions include the nerves connecting the organs of your head to your brain—your eyes, nose, ears, and mouth. They get shortcuts!

As well as passing messages along, your brain stem controls your involuntary muscles, like your heart and some muscles in your stomach. You don't have to remember to tell your heart to beat or let your stomach know when it's time to digest food.

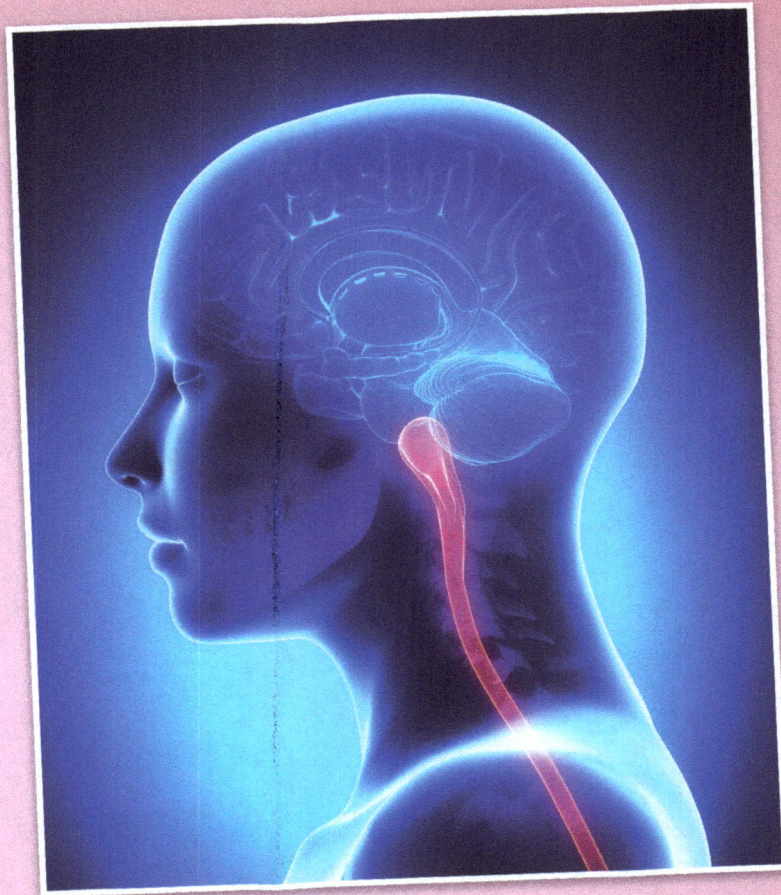

Medulla - female brain anatomy lateral view.

Your brain stem takes care of that so that the rest of your brain can get on with thinking—or even sleeping!

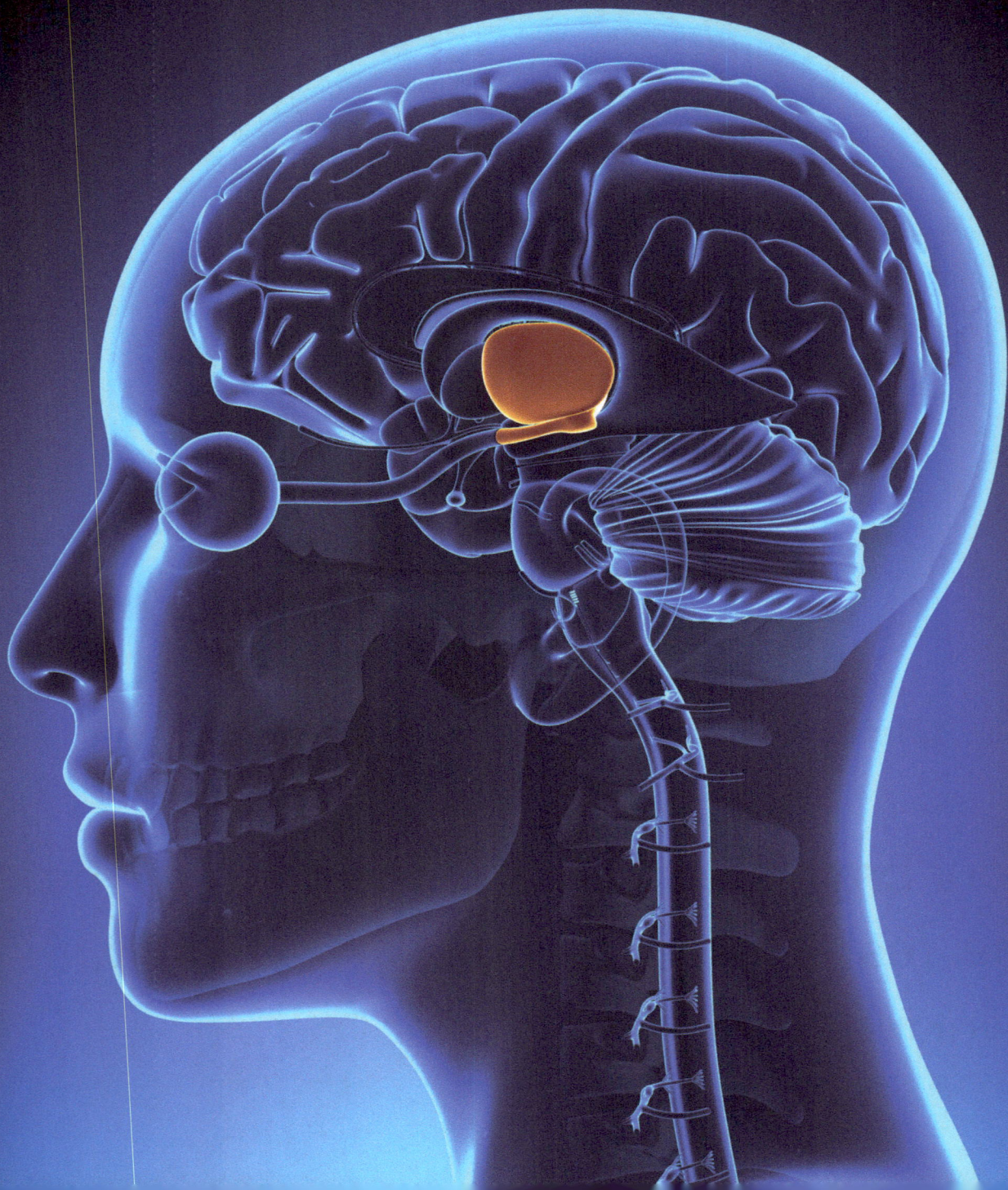

Hypothalamus

Your hypothalamus sits under the center of your cerebrum, just in front of where your cerebrum and your brain stem join. It controls your body's temperature, trying to make sure that your temperature is around 98.6 degrees Fahrenheit at all times. When you get much hotter than that, your hypothalamus tells your body to start sweating so you can cool down. If you get much colder, it tells your body to start shivering to warm you up.

Hypothalamus - female brain anatomy lateral view.

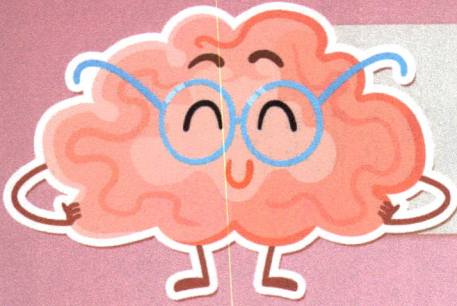

Pituitary Gland

Your pituitary gland is tiny, but it has a big job. It creates and distributes at the right time hormones that your body needs. When you grow, it's because this gland sent growth hormones to your body. When boys and girls become men and women at puberty, the pituitary gland sends out the instructions that start major changes in your body.

Pituitary gland - female brain anatomy lateral view.

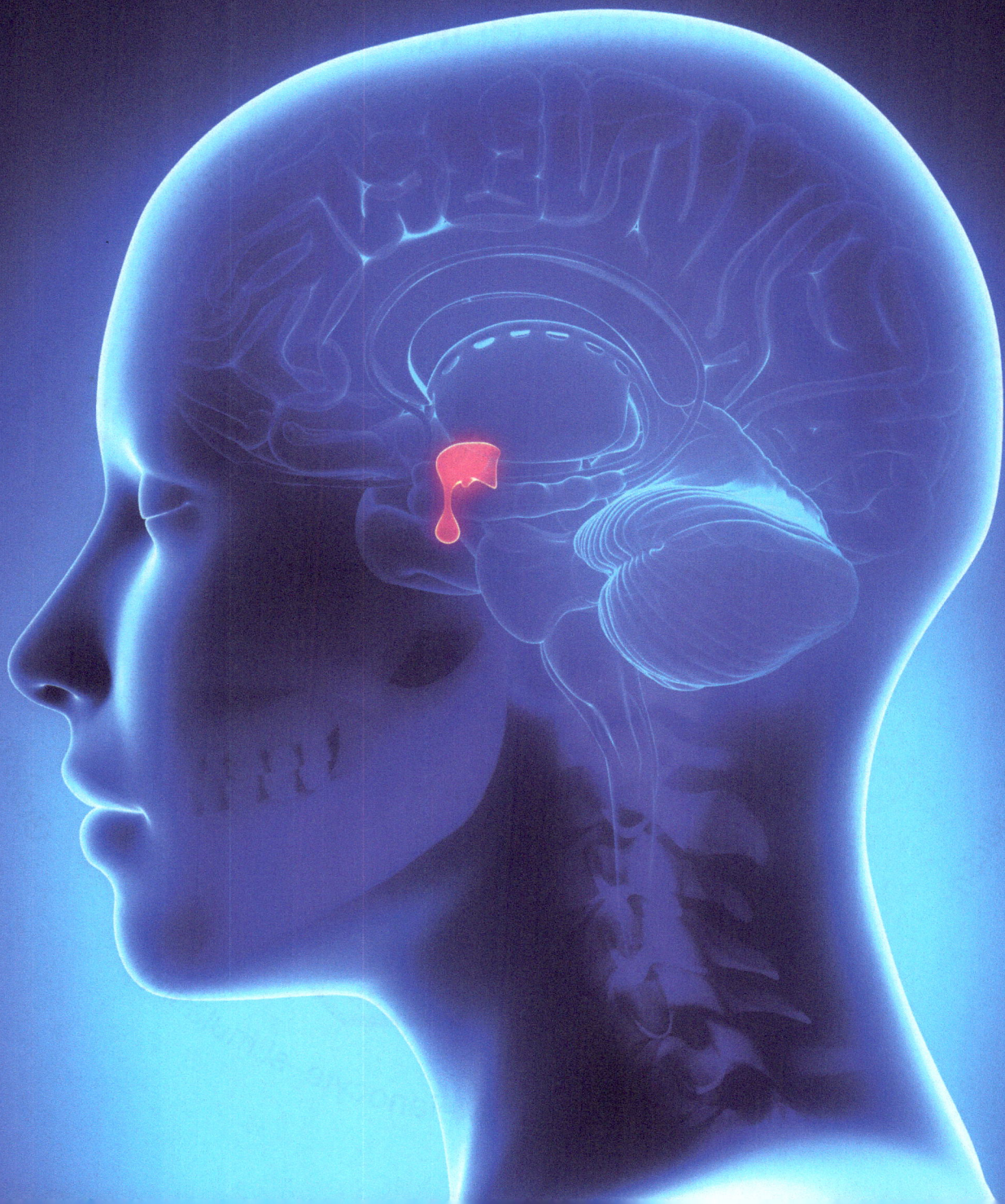

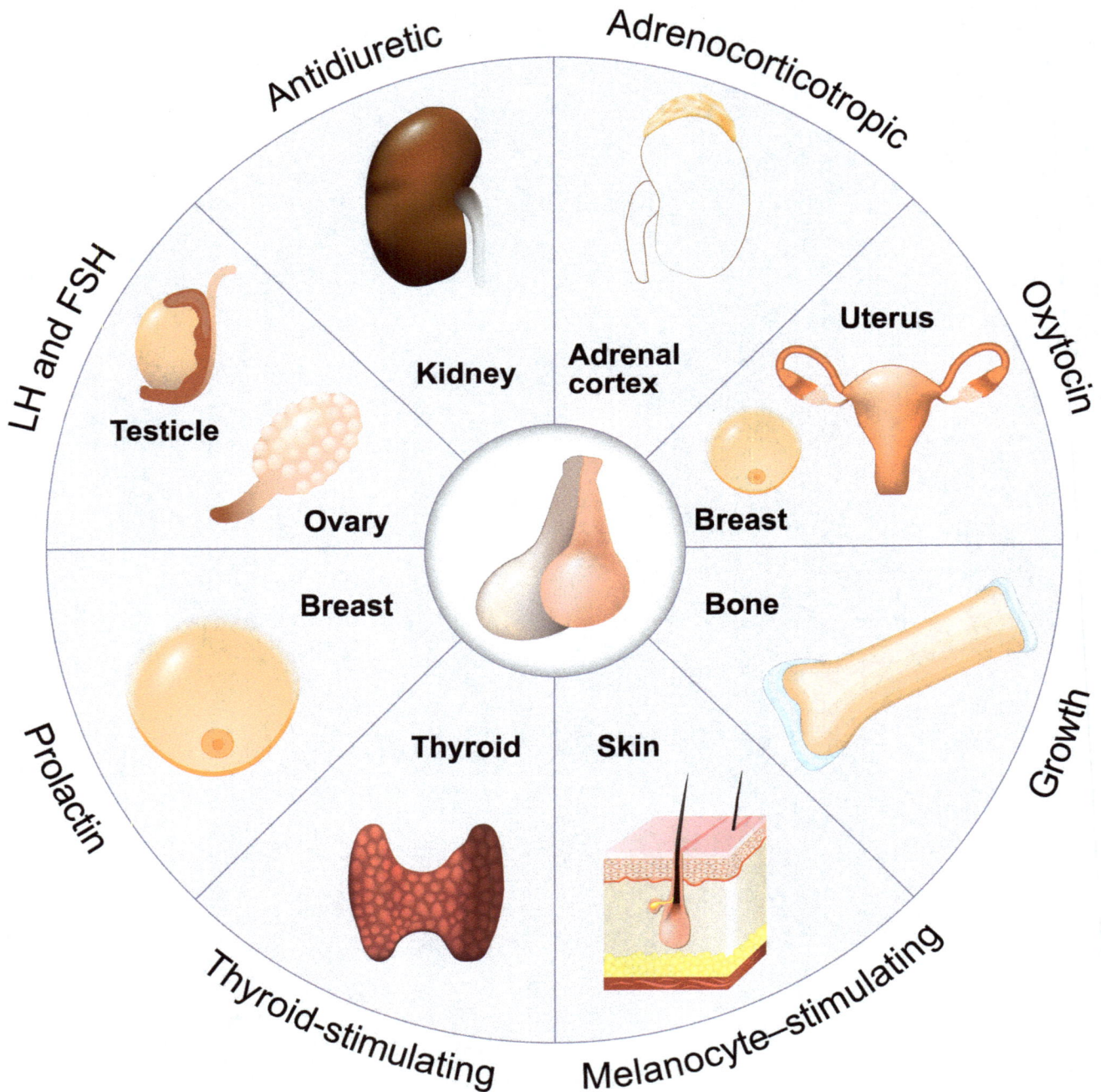

PITUITARY HORMONES

Antidiuretic

Adrenocorticotropic

LH and FSH

Oxytocin

Kidney

Adrenal cortex

Uterus

Testicle

Breast

Ovary

Breast

Bone

Prolactin

Growth

Breast

Thyroid

Skin

Thyroid-stimulating

Melanocyte–stimulating

The pituitary gland hormones also help balance how much water and how much sugar your body has, to keep your systems in balance. Without the help of this gland, you would very soon not feel very well at all.

Summary hormones secreted from the pituitary gland

Amygdala

Your brain is not just about what your body is feeling or making calculations. It is also about what you feel: your emotions. When you are happy or sad or scared or homesick, your amygdala are at work. The amygdala (which is Latin for "almond", because that's their shape!) are little bundles on each side of your brain. They process what is going on around you and in you, and provide a suitable emotion so you can understand the situation and react in an appropriate way.

Amygdala - female brain anatomy lateral view.

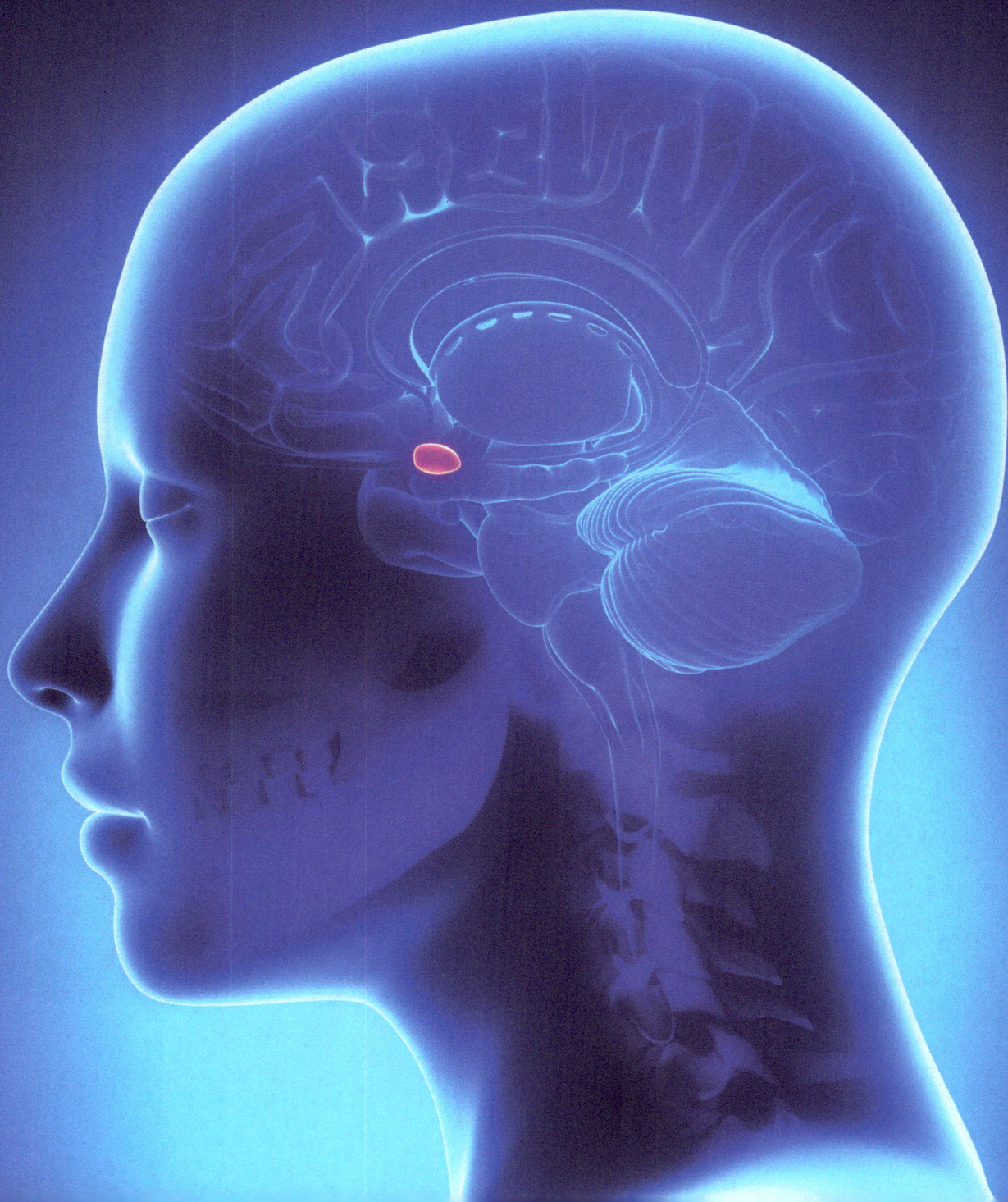

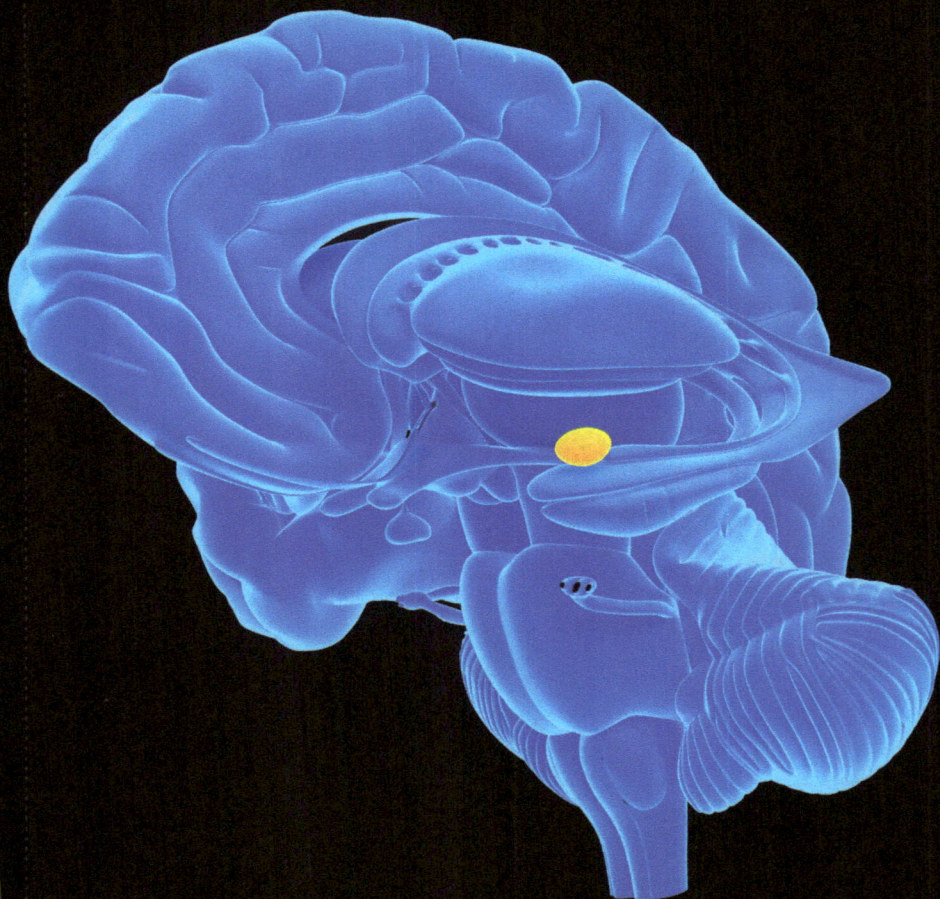

Your amygdala are involved in first impressions. When you meet somebody and, without knowing why, you immediately like them or feel uneasy about them, the amygdala is involved. Your brain has quickly taken everything you know about this new person and checked it against all your memories and conscious knowledge.

The amygdaloid body.

Then the amygdala weighs in and says something like, "The last time you met a guy like this, it did not turn out well," or, "This seems like one of those nice people." First impressions are not always correct, but your brain, and especially your amygdala, are trying to give you the best help possible.

Cross section through the brain showing the limbic system and all related structures.

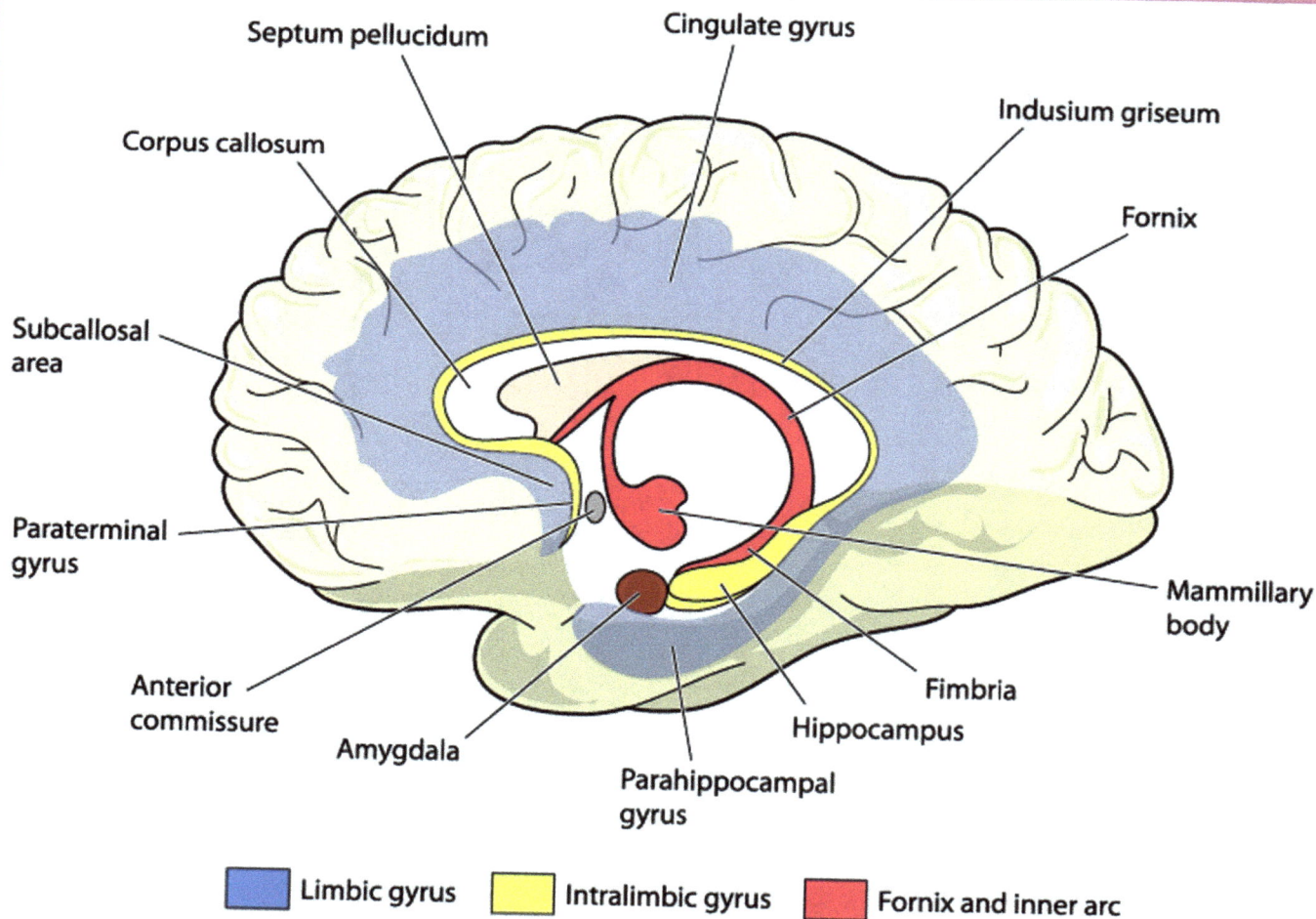

Septum pellucidum

Cingulate gyrus

Corpus callosum

Indusium griseum

Fornix

Subcallosal area

Paraterminal gyrus

Anterior commissure

Amygdala

Mammillary body

Parahippocampal gyrus

Hippocampus

Fimbria

Limbic gyrus   Intralimbic gyrus   Fornix and inner arc

All Those Nerves!

The parts of the brain do wonderful things, but they could not know what to think, or instruct your body about what it should do, without your nervous system. Your nervous system is an information network throughout your body, and the main passage for messages from your body to your brain, and back again, is your spinal cord.

Neurons.

Y ou can't see nerves without a microscope. They are long strands of neurons that can pass messages back and forth through synapses, the connectors between neurons. They are the essential communication tool your brain uses to know what's going on and to stay in control of your body.

Synaptic transmission of the human nervous system.

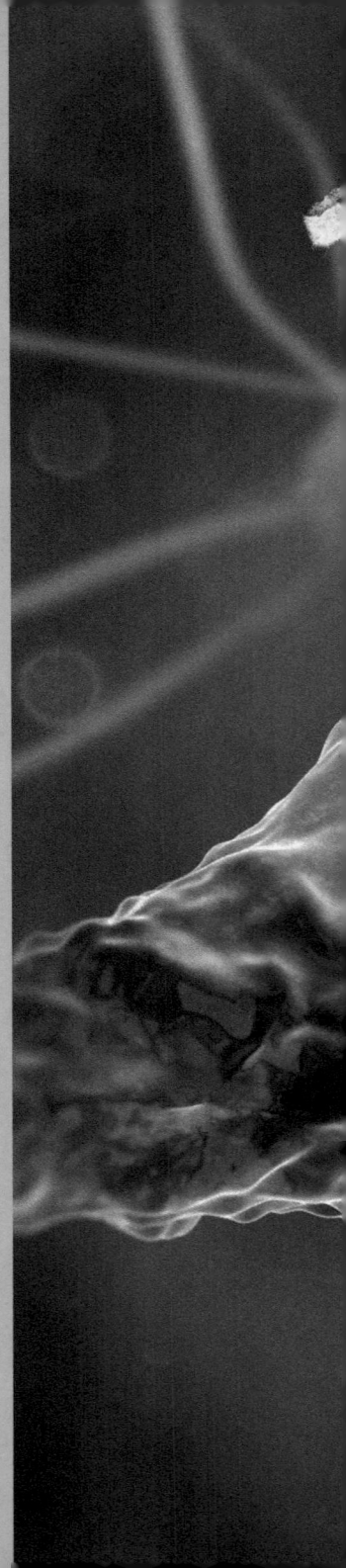

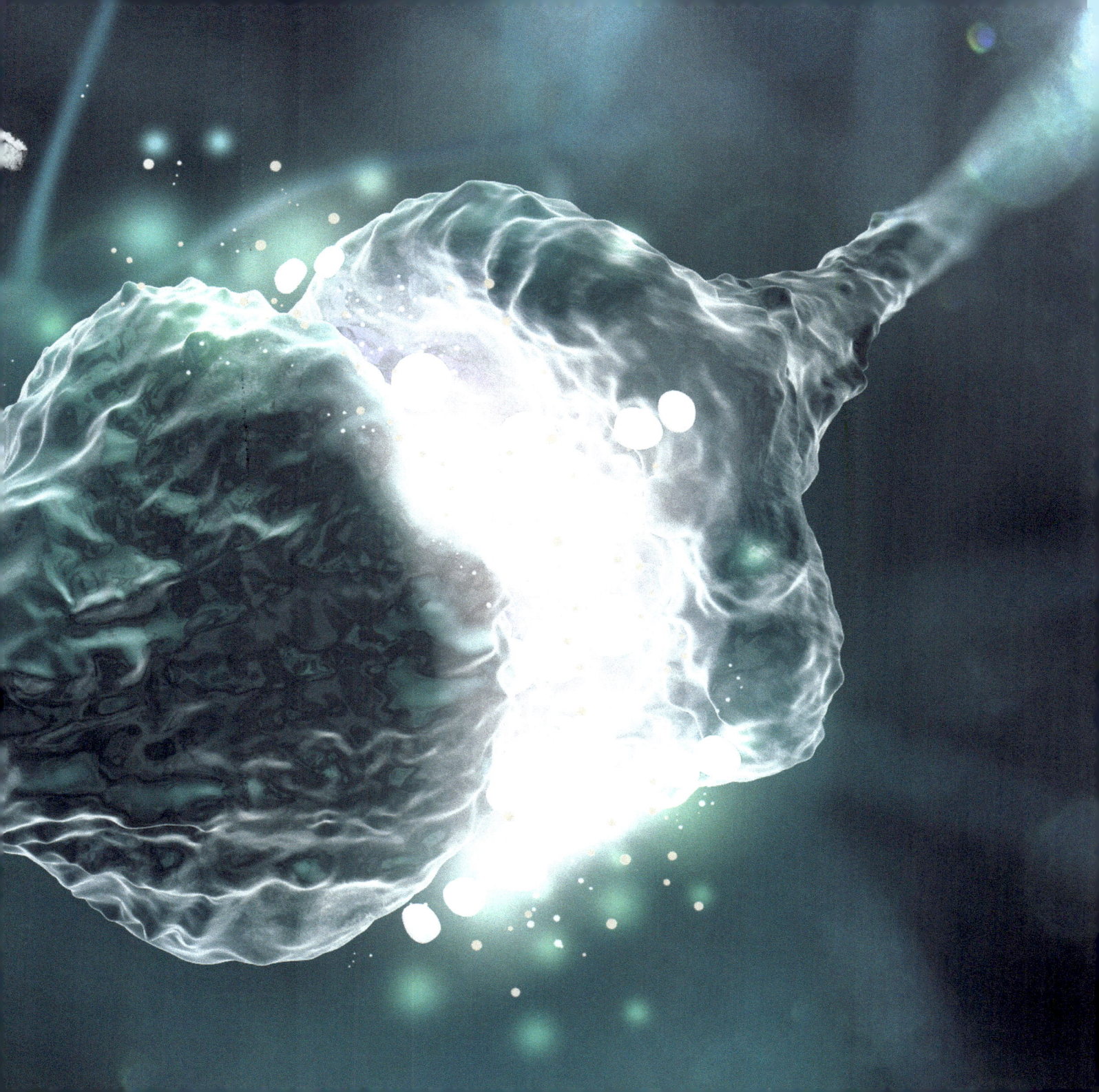

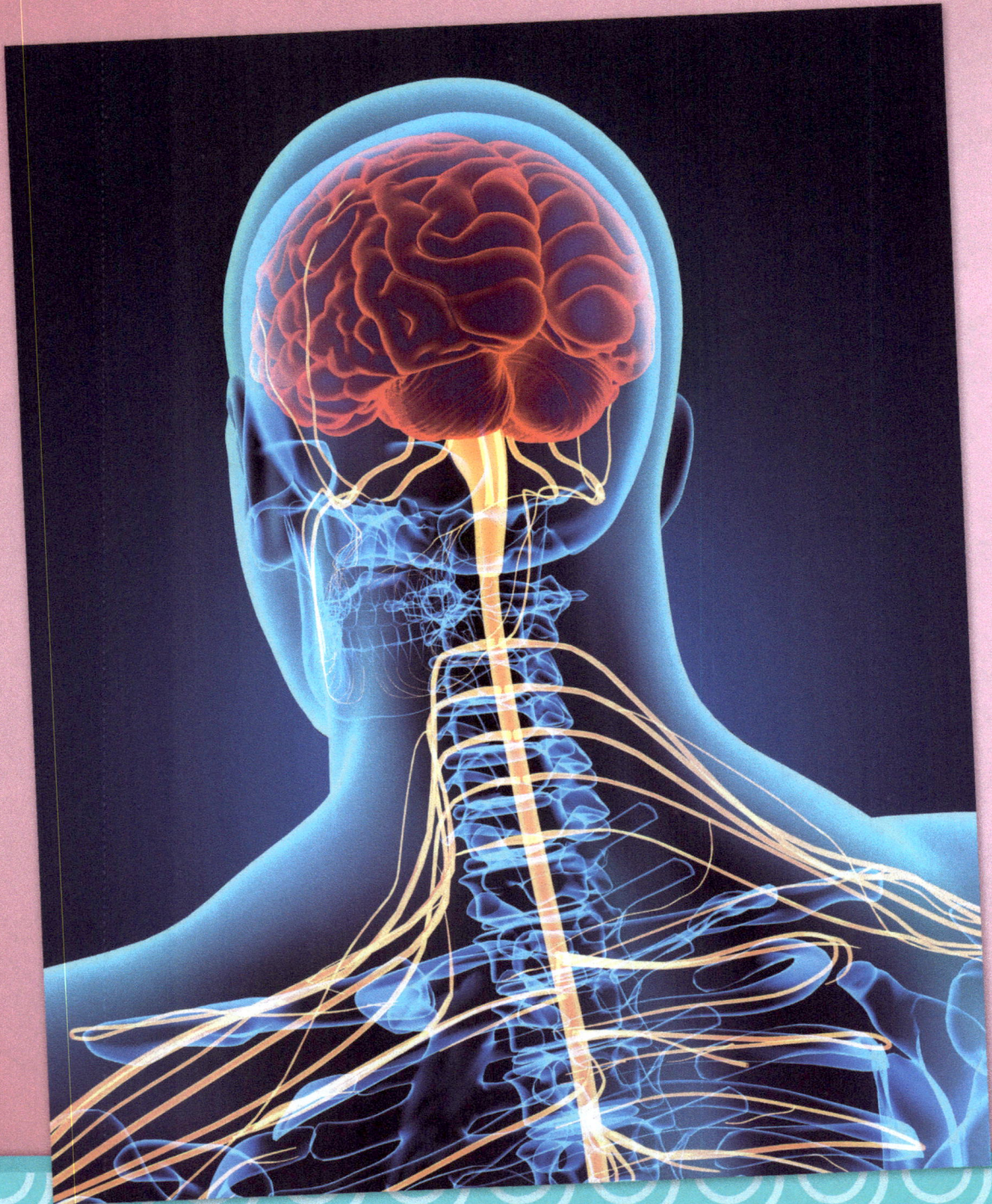

A lot of a baby's neurons are not yet connected to each other. It is harder for neurons that are not connected to "talk" with each other. As you learn things, from how to walk to how to say words, you gain your ability through practice. As you practice, the neurons involved in that activity fire messages to each other over and over. Pretty soon they create a permanent connection, a pathway, to make sending messages more easy. This is what lies behind the saying that "practice makes perfect."

3D illustration of a male nervous system.

There are a lot of things you do every day without consciously thinking about them, from speaking to pulling on your clothes to eating a meal. The neurons involved in those activities have well-established paths of communication.

Active nerve cell.

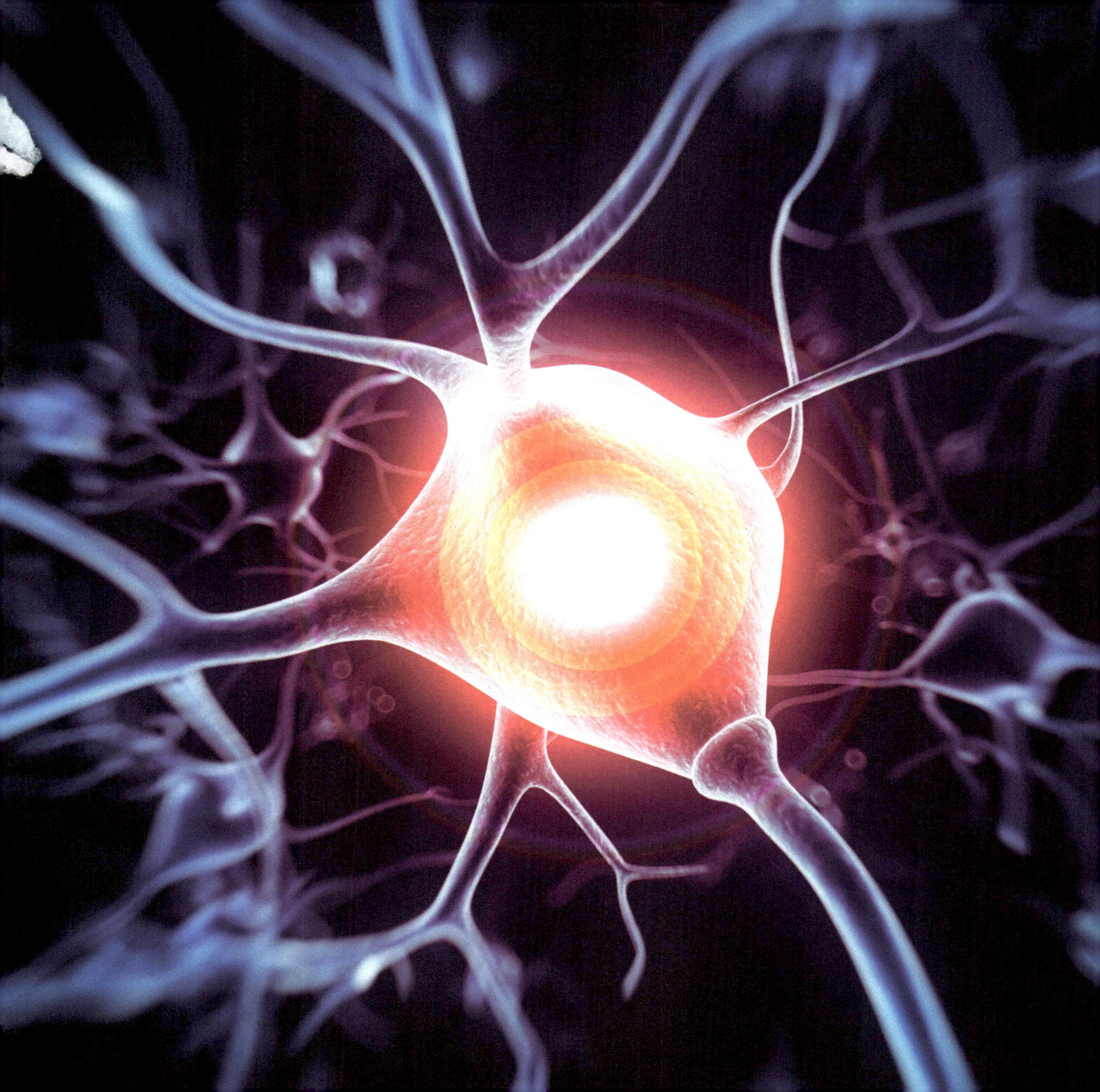

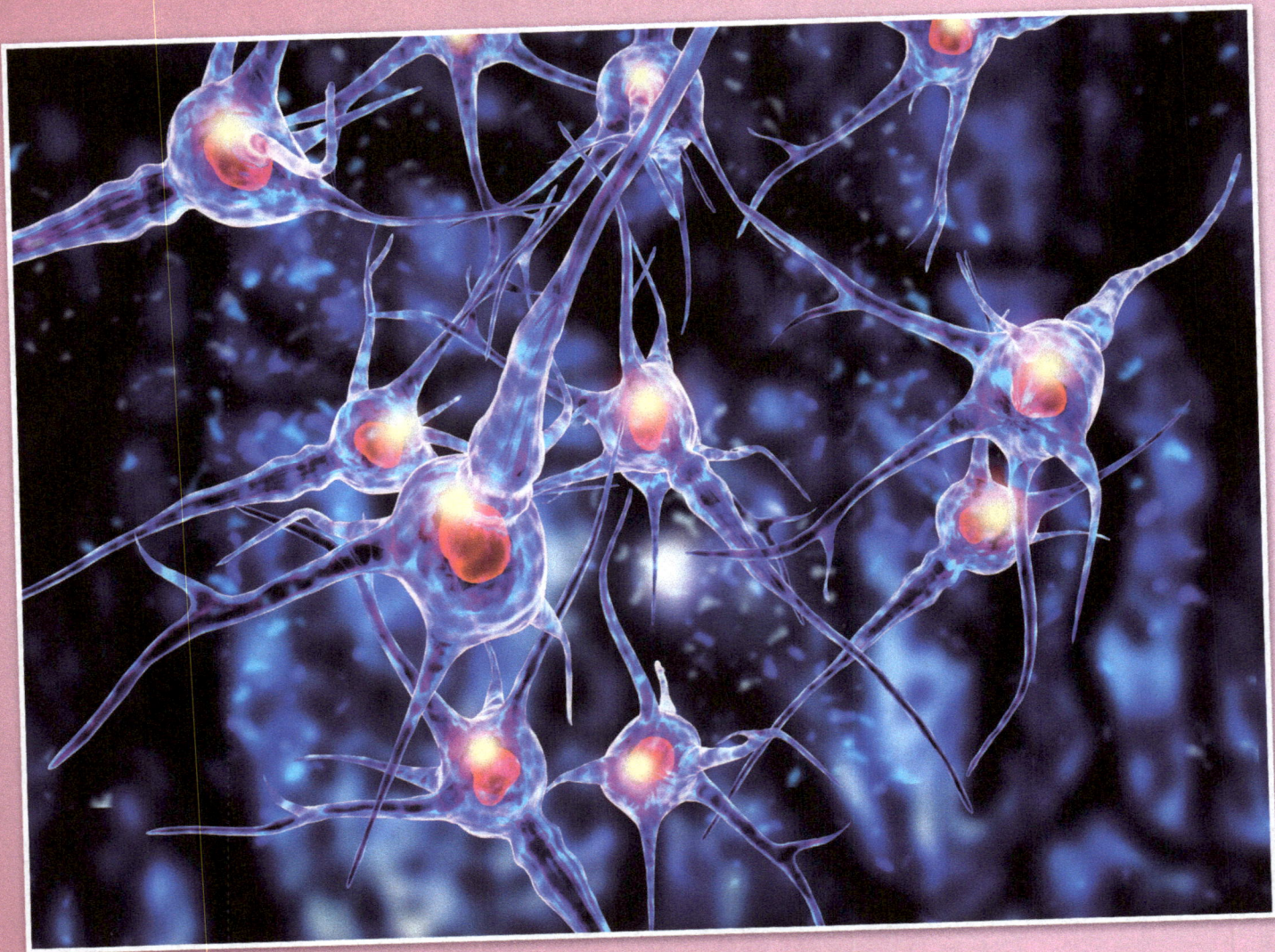

Once you start to take a bite of food, your nervous system and brain can take over and guide you through all the steps of getting the fork into your mouth, getting the food off the fork, getting the fork out of your mouth, and starting to chew without chewing your own tongue, without your making conscious decisions. And you can do all this while listening to someone tell you interesting things: amazing!

3d Illustration of a nerve cell.

Left and right brain functions.

TAKING CARE OF YOUR BRAIN

3d rendering of human brain on technology background

There are things you can do to help keep your brain working well:

- Eat good, healthy food and stay away from junk food. Food with lots of potassium and calcium provides minerals that your brain needs. What it doesn't need is a lot of sugar!

- Exercise a lot. This keeps good pathways open among the neurons that handle movement and balance.

Food for thought.

- Wear a helmet when you're skateboarding or biking or doing other things where you might suddenly fall and whack your head on a wall or the ground. Wearing a helmet may not look super cool, but it is even less super cool if you spend your life with your brain not able to work as you want it to. Read more about this in the Baby Professor book *Concussions: a Football Player's Worst Nightmare.*

MRI image of head showing brain.

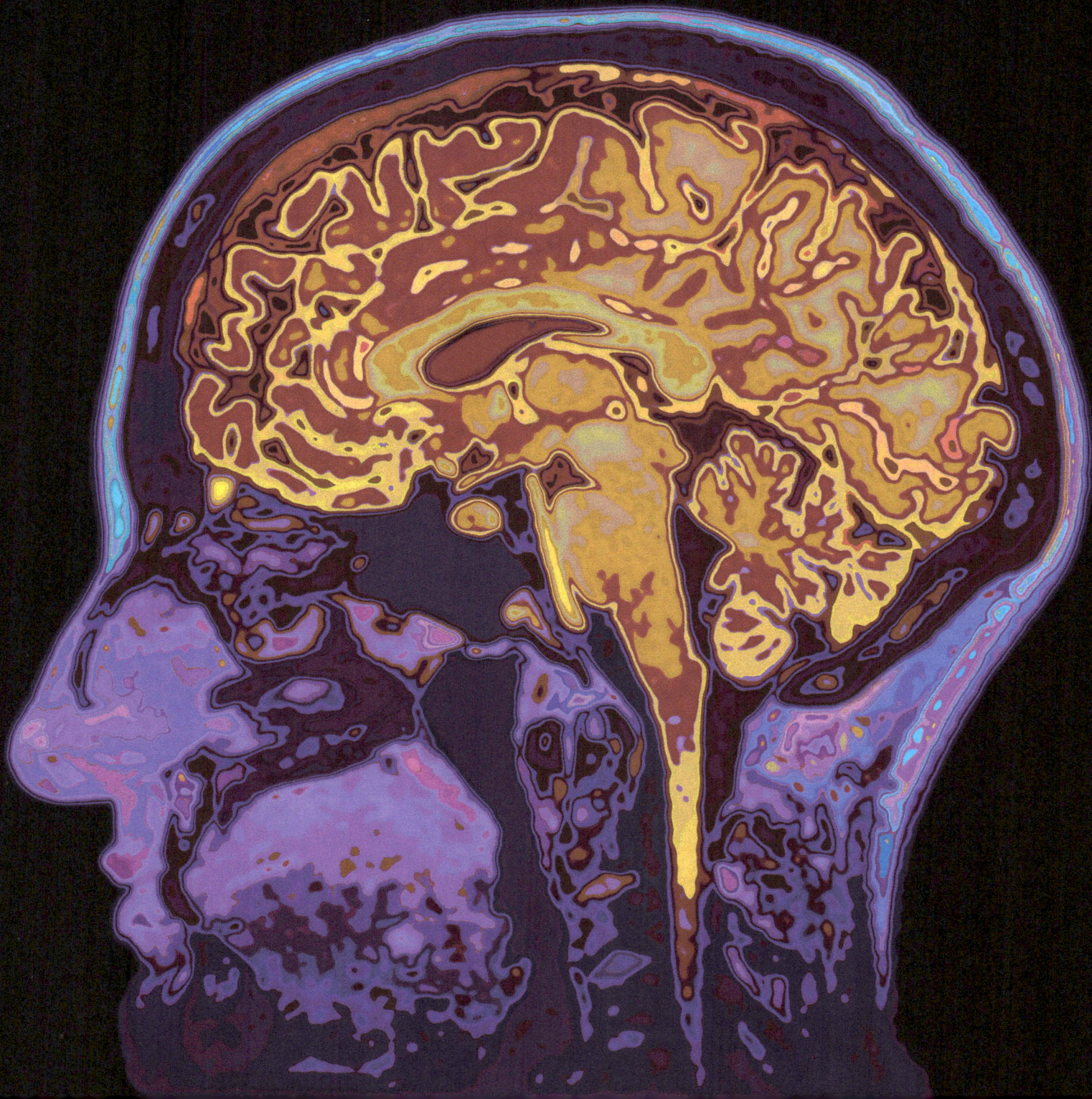

- Stay away from alcohol, tobacco, and drugs, from marijuana right up to the really scary stuff. You need every brain cell you have, and these substances either kill brain cells or break up paths between neurons.

- Challenge your brain: learn new things, especially another language; solve puzzles; read; play music; draw a picture. Every creative activity strengthens existing brain functions and creates new pathways between neurons.

Doctor working with futuristic touch screen interface.

BRAINY BRAIN FACTS

Human brain and neural nerve connections.

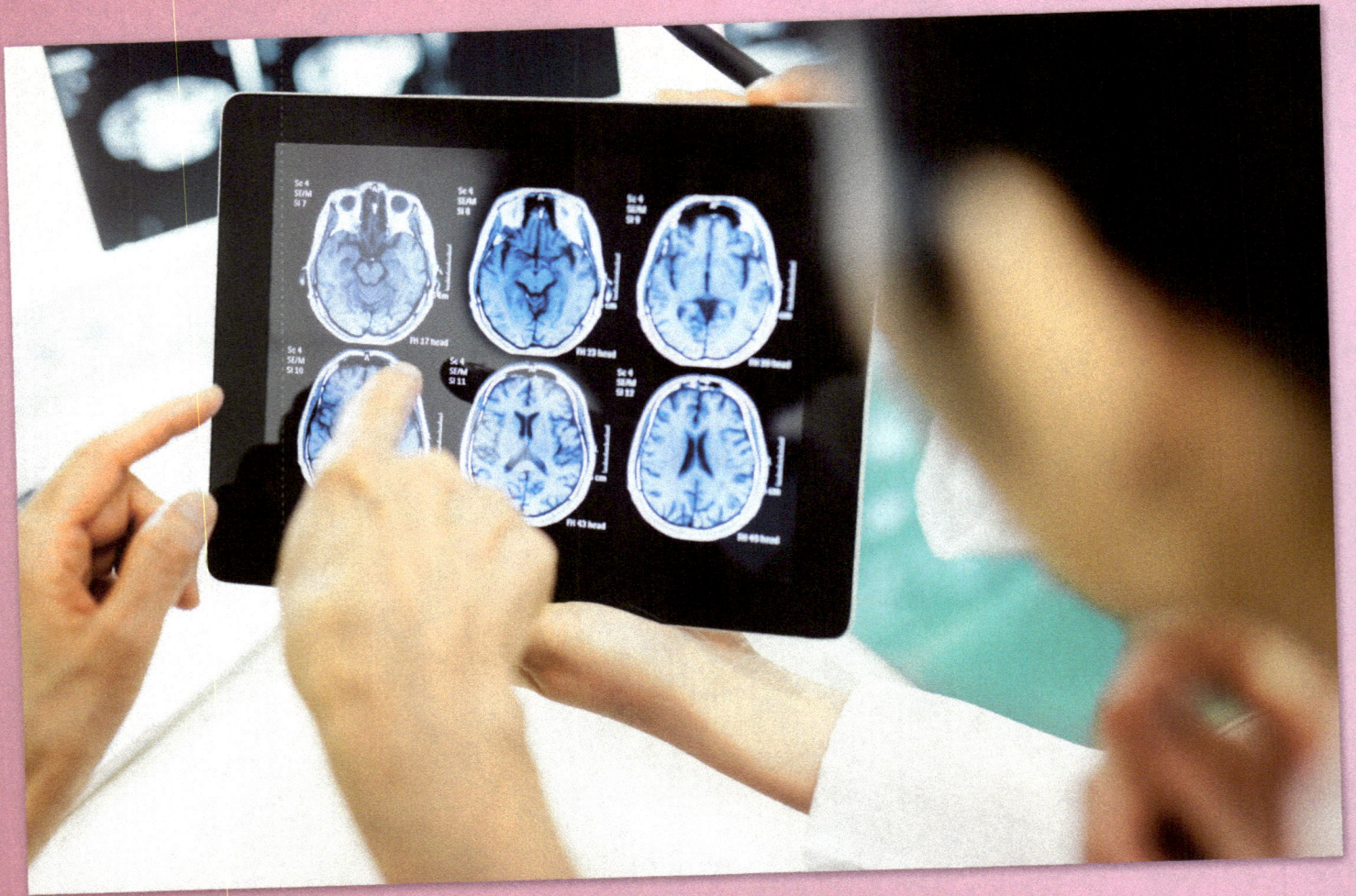

Think About This:

- Although your brain is packed with nerve cells, and part of its job is processing pain messages, like when you stub your toe or cut yourself, the brain itself does not feel pain. When people have brain surgery, they can be awake through the operation without feeling anything that the doctors are doing in their brains.

Doctor and patient using digital tablet in hospital.

- A bit of a brain no larger than a grain of sand has 100,000 neurons, connected to each other with more than a billion synapses.

- When a baby is born, its head is large compared to the rest of its body because its brain is growing very fast. By two years old, a child's brain is 80 percent of its full size.

Little boy and a colorful brain sketch.

- Your brain generates more than 50,000 thoughts every day. Scientists have found that, for a lot of people, more than half of these thoughts are negative-warnings about possible danger, worries about what might happen, or thoughts about bad things that happened in the past.

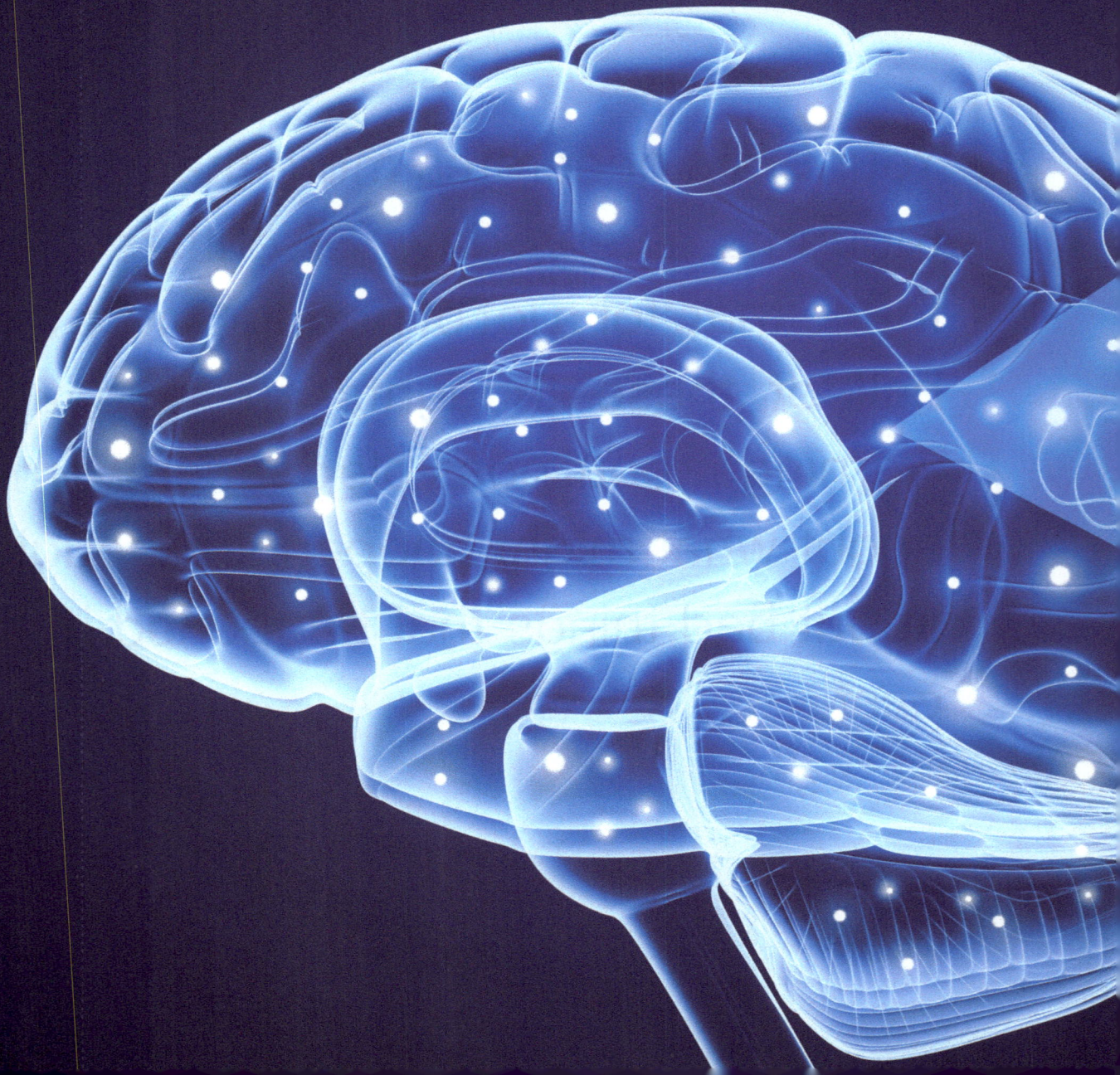
Human brain and active receptor.

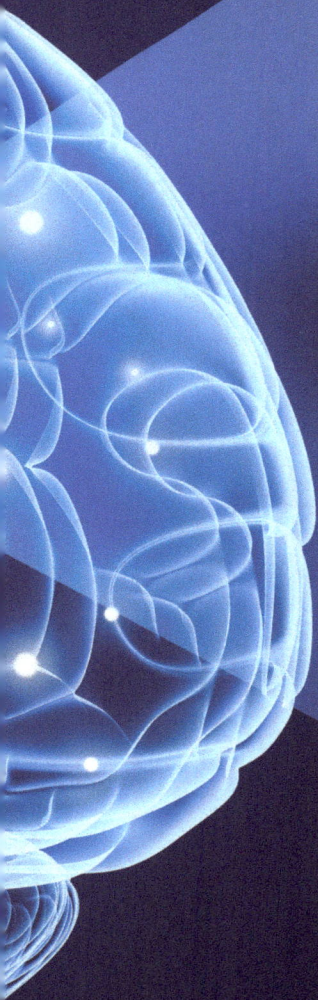

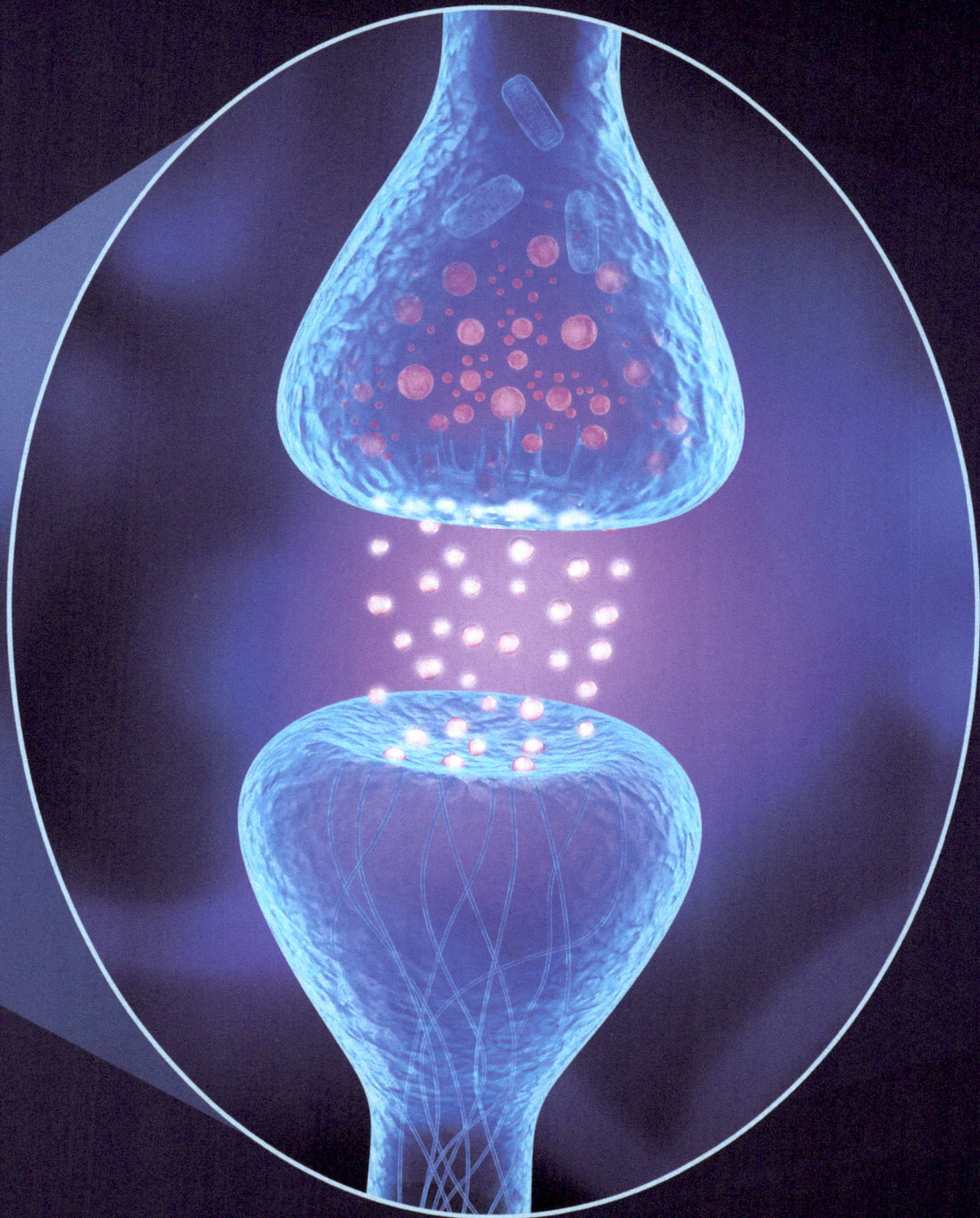

Your Remarkable Body

Your body works hard for you, from your brain down to your toes. Learn more about it in the Baby Professor books Top 50 Quick Facts about the Human Body and I Can Hear, See, Taste, Smell and Feel!

Brain floating on a purple background/thoughts concept.

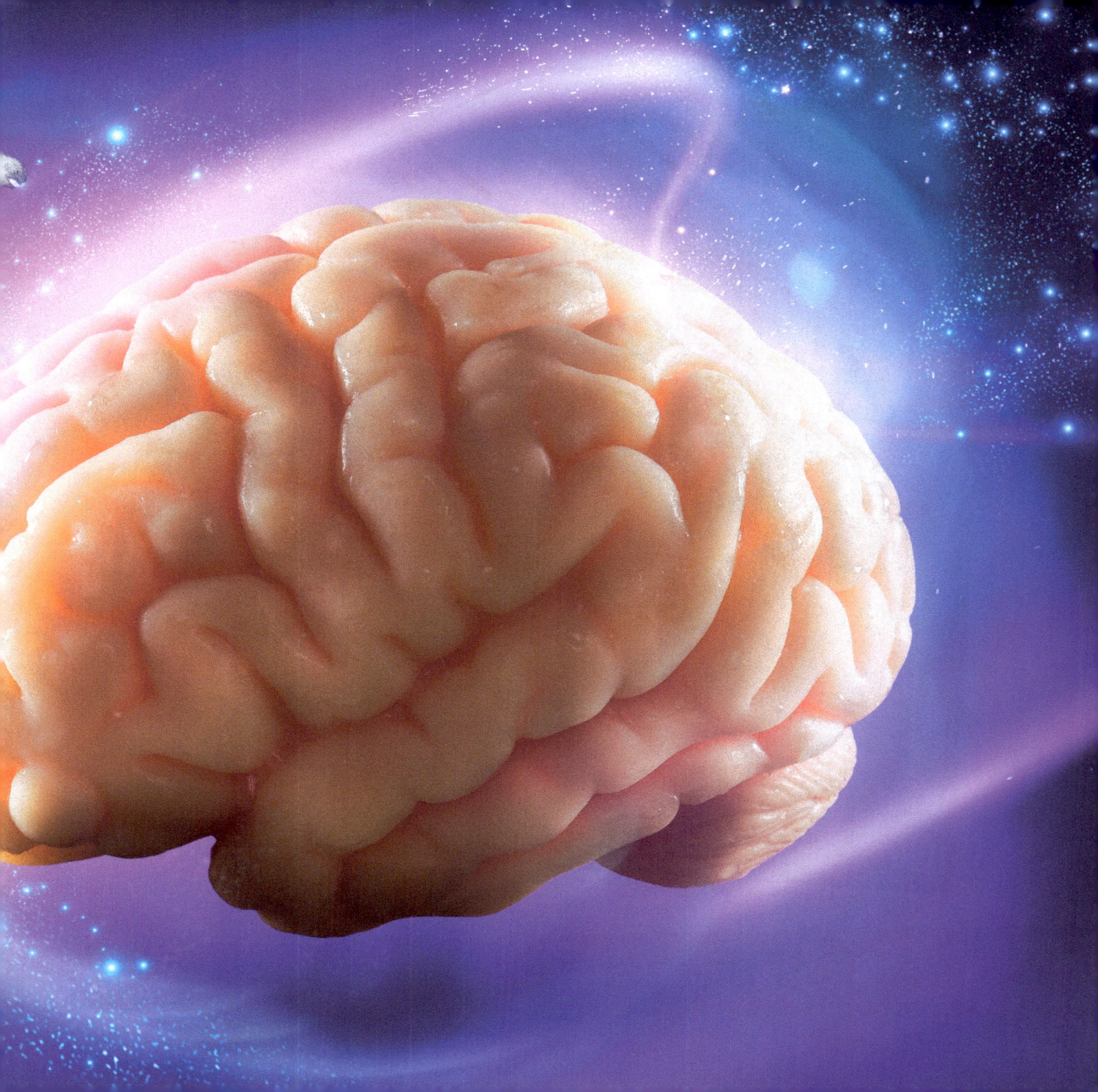

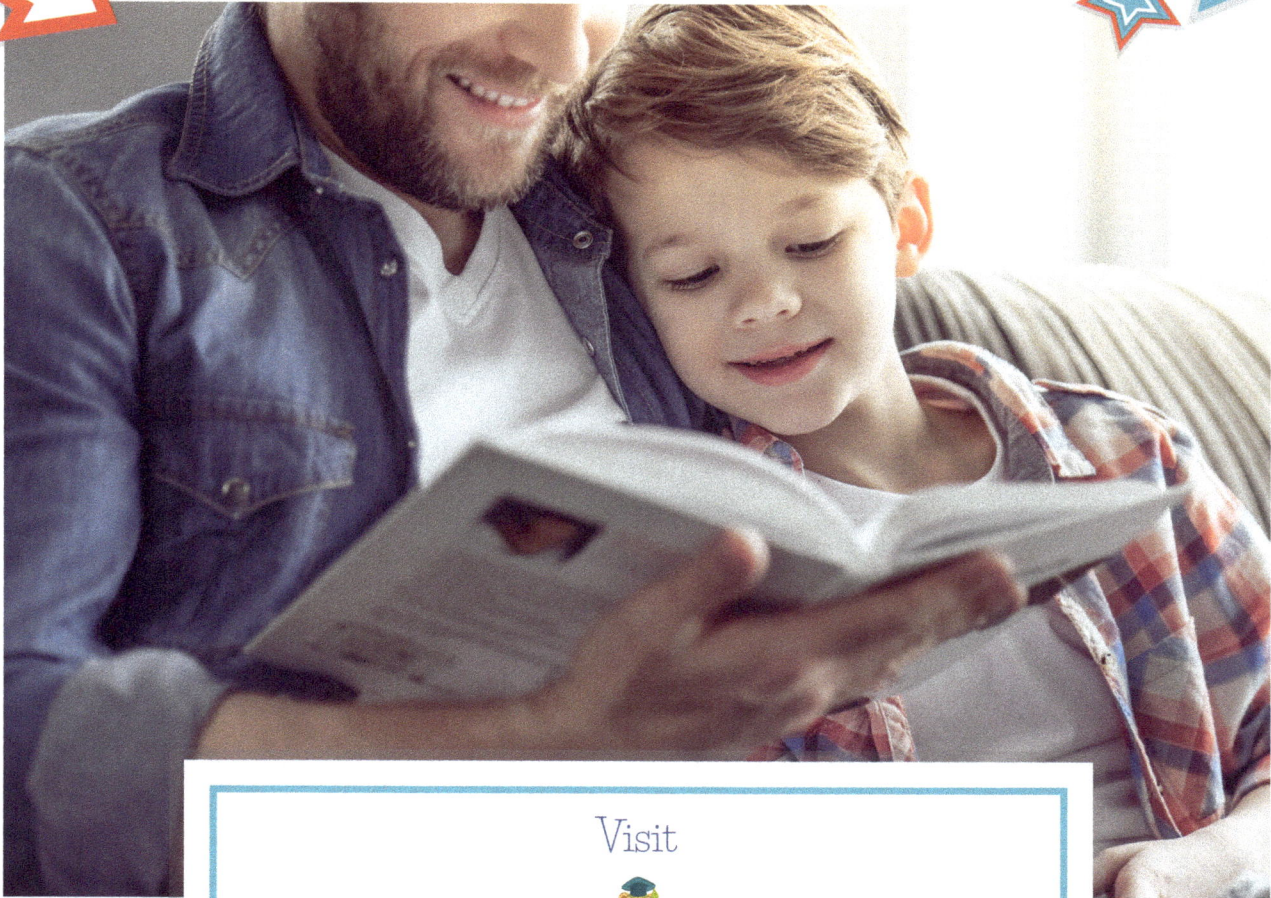

Visit

BABY PROFESSOR
EDUCATION KIDS

www.BabyProfessorBooks.com

to download Free Baby Professor eBooks and view
our catalog of new and exciting Children's Books

Milton Keynes UK
Ingram Content Group UK Ltd.
UKHW051142030924
447802UK00003B/300

9 798869 413499